COGNITIVE BEHAVIORAL THERAPY

A 21 Day Step by Step Guide to Overcoming Anxiety, Depression & Negative Thought Patterns - Simple Methods to Retrain Your Brain

Table of Contents

INTRODUCTION

Congratulations on getting a copy of *Cognitive Behavioral Therapy: A 21 Day Step by Step Guide to Overcoming Anxiety, Depression & Negative Thought Patterns - Simple Methods to Retrain Your Brain*. Anxiety is the most commonly diagnosed mental illness in the world today, and making the decision to give yours the attention it deserves is a big step and one for which you should be rewarded.

It is still just the first step, however, which is where this book comes in. While a structured cognitive behavioral therapy (CBT) program will typically last about four months, there is still plenty of benefit you can see by practicing the same exercises on your own for 21 days. This type of therapy focuses more on breaking bad habits, seeking out negative thoughts, then getting to the absolute heart of your anxiety, which means it is focused on results above all else.

These results are only going to come about with plenty of hard work and determination however, there are no easy fixes here. In the following chapters you will learn all about the basics of CBT before being presented with 21 different exercises. One new exercise is explained each day of the course. While a new exercise is going to be added every day, that doesn't necessarily mean that each exercise is a once done type of thing. It is important to keep each of the exercises up for their recommended period of time in order to get the best results possible. CBT is all about breaking bad habits and replacing them with more productive ones.

There are plenty of books on this subject on the market, thanks again for choosing this one! Every effort was made to ensure it is full of as much useful information as possible, please enjoy!

CBT AND ANXIETY

Imagine for a moment that it is a beautiful Saturday morning. The sky is clear and there is a warm breeze. You have plans later this evening with a group of friends you haven't seen in some time, and you have been looking forward to catching up with them all. It has been a particularly tough few weeks at work and you could use a break. However, as the time for you to leave draws near, seemingly from out of nowhere a sudden onrush of thoughts pour into your brain

What if I do something to embarrass myself? What if things aren't like they used to be? What if they never really liked me and this is all some sort of elaborate prank? Regardless of how much you try and assure yourself that these thoughts are not based on reality, they persist to the point that they cause a physical response. You start to sweat, or maybe your hands begin to shake. Eventually the feeling starts to lessen and now you just feel tired, exhausted even, but still somewhat afraid and on edge.

There may have been a point where you tried to stand up to these thoughts and push them from your mind, knowing you had no real evidence to back any of these worries. However, this assertion likely isn't forceful enough and still leaves room for doubt, so the stream of anxious thoughts continues unabated. Odds are, your stomach starts to turn itself into knots and the fear intensifies, possibly not even in regard to a single thing but rather a mindless, clutching, thing grasping at straws and mewling out of the darkness. As the downward spiral continues you likely lose the strength to defend against the onslaught of anxious thoughts which only become more and more catastrophic the longer they are allowed to proceed unabated.

There is still time before you need to leave to meet your friends, still time to pull yourself together, you think. This idea is quickly subsumed by the anxiety, however, and with a practiced hand you pick up your smartphone and send out a text message to your friends, crying off and begging their forgiveness. You say you're not feeling well, that you're coming down with something, but the truth is you are dealing with anxiety that has run out of control. You avoided the situation, caused your anxiety to retreat, for now, but even still, it likely doesn't abate entirely, it simply sits in the corner, waiting to pounce once more.

If you are lucky enough to not have experienced a variation of the above for yourself, this is an accurate representation of what living with an anxiety condition is like. As everyone experiences anxiety of some sort from time to time, it can be difficult for those with the condition to even be aware that what they are feeling is far beyond what other people feel when they find themselves in a similar situation. The reality of course is, that the anxiety for those with an anxiety condition that impacts on their lifestyle, is like normal anxiety on steroids, stronger, longer lasting and far more damaging.

If you are dealing with this condition it is important to keep in mind that anxiety itself isn't a disease. It is a perfectly useful tool that helped your ancestors avoid danger by priming their flight or fight response to kick in at a moment's notice. An anxiety disorder then magnifies these feelings, causing the person suffering from it to react to these situations far more strongly than those who only deal with a normal amount of anxiety. While a person without these issues might be able to experience anxiety for a brief period of time and then move on, those with an anxiety disorder will dwell on them and be unable to move past this feeling.

What makes anxiety unique is that it is a fear of a potential outcome, almost akin to an obsession with the future. Take the above example, everything that was preventing that person from experiencing life to the fullest was based on assumptions about what may happen at a point in the future. While being curious about the future is one thing, allowing your preoccupation with it to generate an increasing amount of fear within you as a result, is clearly not going to do you any good. What's worse, as the fear inside builds, it likely loses whatever small connection to reality it once had, spinning out often into more and more extreme scenarios, until it seems like the only possible outcome is whatever the worse case scenario may end up being.

The exact trigger for an anxiety disorder can be a complicated or multifaceted question to answer, as disorders are often complicated affairs that are made up of numerous different factors. As such, isolating individual triggers can be difficult, or in some cases even impossible. When you consider all the potential pieces—chemical imbalances in the brain, genetics, side-effects of prescription drugs, substance abuse, environmental factors, and more—it may be best to simply let the root cause go and just accept it on its own.

While classified as a mental illness, anxiety is also known to cause a wide variety of physical symptoms that those who suffer from the condition likely know all too well. In addition to constant feelings of worry or mild distress, anxiety can lead to unfocused or uncontrollable thoughts, obsessive thinking, muscle tension, rapid heartbeat, hyperventilation, sleep issues, stomach pains, headaches, nausea, tremors, shaking and more. When experienced on a regular basis, these symptoms can all combine to essentially retrain your brain to follow less productive or downright harmful patterns in order to deal with the added stressors as best it can, as it is difficult to live with them otherwise.

Over time, this leads to a narrower and narrower band of things that can be dealt with successfully. Unfortunately, in this instance, avoidance does little to help the core issue as the anxiety is based around hypothetical events that have not, and may not, happen. Making things all the more difficult is the fact that those with anxiety often have to deal with feelings of isolation as well. Despite the fact that anxiety disorders are the most commonly diagnosed disorders in the modern world, many people who are dealing with this disorder, find that they have a hard time relating to others with the same issue because it can manifest in so many different ways amongst various individuals.

This feeling of isolation can also occur between the person feeling the anxiety and their friends and loved ones. Without a professional diagnosis, it can be difficult for these people to understand that anything is wrong, as outwardly none of the symptoms are that noticeable unless things proceed past a certain point. As these people have all experienced their own version of anxiety, it can be difficult for them to realize how much more severe the feeling can get.

Finally, it is important to keep in mind that anxiety is a tricky foe to master for many reasons, not the least of which is that he rarely comes alone. A vast majority of anxiety diagnoses are accompanied by other types of issues as well, with depression being the most common. In many ways, many mental health issues can stem from the same source and thus treating one aspect can help in treating them all. There are many different types of treatments for anxiety, but this book is going to focus on a cognitive behavioral therapy (CBT) approach. If the 21-day program outlined in the following chapters doesn't work for you, there are plenty of alternatives out there including traditional medication. It is important to not lose hope and keeping trying to find a way of managing your issues that works for you.

Cognitive Behavioral Therapy

CBT is a type of psychotherapy that focuses on the reasoning that causes you to feel certain ways or perceive certain situations. As anxiety is often caused as a reaction to these things, and because it results in distorted thinking, it can easily warp the way you see the world through flawed perceptions. As such, CBT teaches users a more realistic and healthier way of thinking. CBT is based on a few core principles, the first of which is that thoughts influence actions as well as behaviors, but this is not a one-way street. If you change one component in the cycle, then you influence the others, so you can change all three.

The second principle especially relates to anxiety, as those with extreme anxiety often feel as though they have completely lost control of their lives and everything around them. However, the real problem here is that anxiety tends to cause those who are suffering from it to try and take control of as many of the variables in their lives as possible. CBT teaches users to accept that there are things in life that are always going to be outside of their control and to instead focus their efforts on the things that they can change.

This is largely accomplished through a dedicated process of introspection. CBT is based around the idea that behaviors, feelings and thoughts are all constantly interacting and influencing one another. As such, the way a person thinks or views a specific situation will then ultimately determine how they feel in the moment, which then influences the way they respond as well.

As an example, consider a pair of students who recently both failed the same midterm exam. The first student is positively crushed by the news, their anxiety flares up and they begin to worry that they aren't smart enough to pass the course, what that could mean for their future job prospects and on and on until they feel as though dropping the class is the only rational solution. This, in turn, causes them to develop even more of a negative opinion of themselves while also not making any progress when it comes to fixing the issue that was the problem in the first place. Finally, they develop an overall negative opinion when it comes to their overall level of intelligence, making it less likely that they will take steps to actively fix the actual issue.

On the other hand, the second student, who received the same low grade, feels anxiety at the thought of what the grade will mean for their overall GPA, but is able to get past it by reframing the situation to understand that they simply underestimated the difficulty of the test, or the distribution of the material, and thus did not prepare properly. While this leads to feelings of disappointment, and maybe a little more anxiety, it also ultimately leads to a scenario where future behavior can be improved, to ensure that the grade on future tests improves as well.

The important takeaway here is that the thoughts that you have are a useful means of interpreting the world around you, along with the things that you experience. Everything that you hear, touch, see, smell and taste all provides data that allows your brain to determine what is happening at any given point in time. This is why CBT focuses on the creation of new, positive, habits as these will allow you to more easily interpret the experiences you have in the most positive, and productive ways possible.

This is because a part of any thought is going to involve making assumptions about the stimuli you are presented with. For example, assume you see someone walking towards you holding a knife, while this will not automatically mean that this person means you harm, it is perfectly reasonable to assume that they could be dangerous, until you are presented with a reason to believe otherwise.

Unfortunately, when anxiety comes into play these assumptions can also be extremely harmful and they will just as likely cause you to assume that the person walking towards you is holding a knife when, in reality, they are just reaching for their phone. Those who deal with anxiety tend to experience these instances far more than normal, based on what are known as irrational beliefs.

Due to the fact that each of us is constantly taking in far more information than we can realistically process, a vast majority of the thoughts that you have in response to everyday occurrences are going to occur automatically, without any conscious brainpower being used to generate them. These are known as automatic thoughts and those with anxiety often experience that anxiety bleeding over into their automatic thoughts, heightening the level of anxiety felt overall.

This is because, when an automatic thought occurs, it moves forward without allowing you the opportunity to assess its overall legitimacy and before you are even fully aware what is happening. This causes the brain to automatically accept it as truth, and start to act on it, regardless of whether or not it is based on factual evidence. When a thought is both irrational and automatic it can cause you to experience negative emotions, despite not actually having any reason to feel the way you suddenly do.

Thoughts typically lead to emotions, either directly or indirectly. If you think back to the man with the knife example, you can either automatically assume that this person has negative intentions, which in turn leads to nervousness, fear and anxiety, or you can assume that they have a legitimate reason for doing what they are doing and act appropriately, which is to say take no action and behave normally.

CBT tends to focus on six primary emotions that can occur at various degrees of intensity, and in various combinations, to create the full spectrum of emotions that you are familiar with. These emotions are fear, anger, sadness, surprise, love and joy. When you experience these emotions, the body goes through a wide variety of noticeable physiological changes. If the emotions you are feeling are negative, then you may experience a flight-or-fight response, which in turn can lead to an increased heart rate, along with an overall tensing in the muscles and an increase in sweating.

Despite the fact that they can have a serious effect on your actions, both positive and negative, emotions typically go unnoticed in the moment, in much the same way that automatic thoughts are often treated. This is why it is so important to understand that while your emotions might occur outside of your immediate awareness, they can still have a very real affect on both your behaviors and your subsequent thoughts.

Once you have an emotional reaction to a thought that has been generated as the result of a specific trigger, you will likely find that you are responding to the situation whether you want to or not. This multi-step process is constantly taking place but is rarely interesting enough to warrant additional examination. Unfortunately, if you are dealing with a level of anxiety that far surpasses normal, then these behaviors are far more likely to hurt you than they are to help you.

For example, consider the two students from the earlier example. After their bad day, they both call a friend to hopefully make plans to drown their sorrows. When their friend doesn't answer the phone, the first student, who is suffering from anxiety, automatically assumes the worst and thinks that their friend has abandoned them, and that their entire friendship has been a lie. Meanwhile, the second student assumes that their friend is busy and will call them back when they have the time.

The thoughts that you have in any situation are always going to be influenced by what are known as your core beliefs. These are going to be thoughts that you hold in a much higher regard than anything else you come across, so much so that they can be thought of as the lens that determines how you perceive the world. For those with a high level of anxiety, their core beliefs may look something like this:

- The world is generally a dangerous place

- Everything will always work out for the best

- People are mostly good

- I am unlovable

Your core beliefs are not something that you come to overnight, rather they develop over a prolonged period of time, based on the experiences that you have had in your own life. Unfortunately, just because you drew a specific conclusion from a certain experience, doesn't mean that it is the right one. Indeed, it could be the completely opposite lesson from how things work in the world. While having core beliefs that are a little out of whack isn't normally that serious, for those with a high level of anxiety, their beliefs can make the world seem far more dangerous and complicated than it really is.

Your core beliefs can be thought of as a series of filters that each of your thoughts, even your automatic thoughts, must pass through in order for them to then interact with your emotions and actions. For example, if you have a core belief that tells you that you are unlovable, then even if you spend the day with a friend and have a lovely time, you will find yourself questioning the legitimacy of the friendship and whether the other person is simply spending time with you because they feel sorry for you; you are, after all, unlovable so there must be some ulterior motive in play.

Faulty core beliefs often lead to negative thought patterns that are collectively known as cognitive distortions. These then often end up reinforcing existing negative emotions and thoughts. These are often especially common in those with elevated levels of anxiety and tend to manifest themselves in a variety of harmful ways.

Emotional reasoning: This type of cognitive distortion is commonly based around the assumption that the way emotions cause a person to see the world is actually an accurate depiction of the way it really is.

Fortune telling: This type of cognitive distortion is commonly based around the assumption that a specific upcoming situation is going to end poorly, despite having a complete and utter lack of evidence indicating that this is the case.

Mind reading: This type of cognitive distortion is commonly based around the assumption that what you consider that others are thinking or feeling about you is the way they are actually feeling about you.

Personalization: This type of cognitive distortion is commonly based around the assumption that you are directly responsible for things that are far outside of your control.

Overgeneralization: This type of cognitive distortion is commonly based around the assumption that every time you experience a specific event or activity it will turn out the same as your sole frame of reference.

Catastrophizing: This type of cognitive distortion is commonly based around the assumption that the worst possible outcome is going to occur regardless of any evidence to the contrary.

Minimization and magnification: This type of cognitive distortion is commonly based around the assumption that positive things that happen to you don't matter while the negative things that happen to you take on an importance far beyond what is actually justified.

Magical thinking: This type of cognitive distortion is commonly based around the assumption that two completely unrelated events are actually related.

DAY 1

JOURNALING

In order to get started with CBT successfully, the first habit that you are going to need to build is going to be based around writing down all of the things that you feel anxious about through the day. By putting your thoughts down on paper, you will give them a tangible structured form that will in many cases be easier to deal with directly rather than having them running around in your head in an unorganized manner. This won't be a simple diary where you record your standard comings and goings. However, you are going to want to set your journal up in a specific fashion to ensure that it is able to allow you to explore your thoughts in the proper way. You are going to want to start your journal today and continue writing in it indefinitely.

This exercise will surely prove helpful in a variety of ways such as:

Improving your ability to express yourself: If you have ever tried to express yourself when it comes to explaining your anxiety to someone else, you likely found it to be far more difficult than you would like. This is because it is often difficult to articulate why something makes you worry, especially in the moment. As such, by laying your thoughts out on a piece of paper, you can practice how you communicate with others.

Self-reflection: As you become more aware of yourself and the cycles your thoughts tend to go through, it can be easy for certain thoughts to get lost in the shuffle. If you have a written record of your thoughts on hand however, it can act like a map that shows where you have been, making it easier for you to determine where you want to go. You will be able to see the types of thoughts you had on specific days and more importantly see that what you were so afraid of rarely (if ever) actually came to pass.

Getting started: When setting up your journal you are going to want to create five separate columns labeled situation, thoughts, emotions, behaviors and alternatives. In the column for situation, you are going to want to describe the experience you had with no emotion attached. Facts are key here as any personal bias at this stage will only skew things further out of line.

In the thought column, you are going to want to include the thoughts that the experience in question caused you to have. These may be either questions or statements, but the most important thing is to be honest with yourself about these in what you write down, recording anything but what is really going on will prove to be counterproductive in the end. When it comes to emotions, you are going to want to include a simple and concise explanation of how the experience made you feel.

In the behaviors column you are going to want to chronicle how you responded to the situation in the moment. It is important to make sure that you write down how you actually responded in the situation, not how you wish you responded. You are also going to want to include how your actions affected the situation as well. Finally, in the column for alternative thoughts you are going to want to list thoughts you could have had instead, that would have lead to less of an anxious outcome.

DAY 2
MINDFULNESS MEDITATION

While it has been a part of countless religious rituals for thousands of years, mindfulness meditation has only caught on in the West in recent decades, thanks to its proven ability to improve mental health in a wide variety of ways, including treating anxiety. Since its inception, mindfulness meditation has been proven via scientific study to improve the physical wellbeing of those that practice it on a regular basis. At its heart, mindfulness meditation is all about focusing your mind to ensure that you are as fully aware of each moment as possible. This, in turn, allows you to exist more completely in any given moment by expanding your consciousness to the fullest.

The end result is that you are able to exhibit greater control over your thoughts as a whole, something that can be exceedingly useful when you feel an anxiety attack closing in on you. While this might sound practically impossible at first, being mindful is a skill, which means that it can be improved with practice, just like any other one. Practicing is easy as well. All you need is 15 minutes and someplace quiet to start with, though eventually you will be able to practice mindfulness meditation virtually anywhere. This is another activity that you are going to want to start today and keep up indefinitely. In addition to the mental health benefits it can offer, it is also proven to provide a wide variety of physical health benefits as well.

Getting started

When you are first getting started with mindfulness meditation, it is important to find a time that will be easily repeatable. If your body can get into the habit of entering a mindful state at approximately the same time every day, then you will likely find the overall process much more manageable. Keep in mind that it takes about a month for a new habit to become a part of your routine, as long as you can keep it up for that long, the rest will be easy.

In order to reach a state of mindfulness, you are going to want to find someplace comfortable and quiet to sit, though not so quiet and comfortable that you are tempted to fall asleep. Then, all you need to do is breathe deeply, in and out. As you breathe in, focus all of your attention on the information that your senses are providing to you. Focus on the way the air feels in your lungs, how it smells and how it tastes. Slowly but surely, expand your consciousness so that you are taking in as much information about your surroundings as possible.

When you can reach a point where you are thinking about nothing except what is happening right now, then you have experienced a state of mindfulness. If you find yourself having a hard time reaching that point, you may have success picturing yourself staring at a stream of bubbles flowing by, each one representing a thought. If you find yourself being drawn into interacting with a specific thought, simply visualize it floating away instead.

DAY 3
BEHAVIORAL ACTIVATION

Behavioral activation is an exercise that works based on the idea that if enough negative life events are piled onto your plate over time, you may not experience the level of positive reinforcement required to react appropriately in all situations. This can lead to an unwarranted feeling of anxiousness, in addition to social withdrawal, erratic behavior and any number of negative outcomes.

If this is the case, then the best way to counteract this negative build up of influences is to instead find something that you are good at and then find a way that you can show off this talent in a setting that will ensure that you receive the praise you both need and deserve. While many people will read this exercise, and feel as though they don't have the types of performance based skills that are required for such an endeavor, the skill that you choose to show off doesn't need to be anything nearly so limiting.

Everyone has skills that they are good at, even if they aren't flashy or easily appreciated at a glance. If you can't think of anything off hand, then you are likely thinking about the question in the wrong way. Simply start by considering the things that you do regularly that easily come to you, such as cooking a meal for the family or completing a word puzzle.If you explore these daily activities more thoroughly you will likely discover that. you have mastered something over the years that will often leave others dumbfounded.

Once you have found your special talent, the next thing will be to find a place to put it to use in a way that other people will see and recognize your abilities. Again, this doesn't need to be performance based. If your skill is in organizing or planning for example, then finding a charity to work with and helping to plan an event for them could be a great choice. If you are a good cook but mostly cook for yourself, invite your friends over for a fancy meal. Regardless of what your skill is, you should be able to find a way to show it off, as long as you put a little thought into it.

Finally, once you find an activity that serves to boost your confidence, keep it up. While you might not feel a big change in your overall level of anxiety at first, you will be surprised what feeling confident about one aspect of your life can do for your overall confidence levels, and likewise what being more confident in general can do for your feelings of anxiety. Once you find this type of positive outlet, you are going to want to make boosting your confidence a normal part of your daily routine.

DAY 4
AFFIRMATIONS AND MANTRAS

Anxiety is triggered by the way you perceive situations that you have previously been in and those that are on the horizon. These perceptions are, in turn, influenced by the filters that your mind has built up over time, based on the data it has recorded from the experiences you have had so far. When you find yourself thinking through a negative type of filter you will likely only see the negative aspects of a given situation, regardless of the positive ones that existed at the same time. If you chronically see every glass as half empty, then you may have an issue with negative filters.

In fact, if your anxiety gets bad enough, your filters will likely go so far as to remove all of the calming and positive aspects of your day, so all you can see is the things that make you anxious, compounding the problem and making it seem as though there is no way to solve it. This is where affirmations and mantras come in, as the repetition that comes along with them is a great way to bypass these filters and allow your mind to let in some new (hopefully more positive) thoughts for a change.

An affirmation is simply a positive sentence that you write down multiple times throughout the day. A mantra is the same sentence, just repeated in your mind instead of written down. They are both a great way to quiet the mental background noise that is created by your anxiety and to eventually retrain your brain, bypassing the existing negative mental filters in the process.

Examples include:

- Today, you are perfect

- Forward progress! Just keep moving!

- You are the sky

- I am attracting all the love I dream of and deserve

- Follow my path to happiness

- I am strong. I am beautiful. I am enough

- I am grateful for my life so far and for what is to come

- I am fulfilled

When you first start this exercise, which you are going to want to continue every day, indefinitely, it is likely that your mind is going to respond negatively to the process, after all, the saying you are using should fly directly in the face of your established mental filters. This is perfectly natural, however, and in no way indicates the level of success you will have with this exercise as a whole. Rather, it is important to remember that your negative filters have built up over years, if not decades, which means that you aren't going to find success overnight. As long as you keep it up, however, you will be able to move in the right direction.

You will know that you have found success when you can hear your mantra playing in the background of your mind, even when you are not consciously thinking about it. If you are instead writing your affirmations down, make an effort to do so at least five times per day.

DAY 5

BREATHING EXERCISES

A major aspect of CBT is the fact that thoughts influence behaviors and feelings, in addition to playing a large role in determining our overall wellbeing. As such, treating your anxiety successfully is likely going to require a physical, as well as a mental component. For example, think back to your last anxiety attack, specifically the way you felt physically. How did you feel in the moment? How did these feelings change as the attack persisted?

Of all the physical symptoms that are known to come along with anxiety, poor breathing has the potential to be the most damaging, simply the way in which we breathe directly effects the way our bodies function. When you are anxious, your breathing may increase dramatically or slow to a crawl, the specifics don't matter as either receiving too much oxygen or too little can exacerbate other symptoms, generating a snowball effect and making the overall experience much worse than it would otherwise be.

Luckily, you can learn to control your breathing with, what should be relatively little practice. Once you have gotten the hang of this exercise, you won't need to practice it every day, only at points where you feel a serious need to do so.

In order to get started, all you need to do is find a comfortable place to sit, and ensure that you are wearing clothing that is not restrictive. Sit up, with your back straight, and breath in slowly for a total of four seconds. You will then want to hold that breath for seven seconds, before exhaling again for a total of eight seconds. You are going to want to repeat this process for about two minutes, though you can extend it to four minutes if you don't feel the effects right away. You may also find success if you close your eyes during the process, though some people prefer to look at what is causing their anxiety instead.

As you repeat this exercise, you will likely notice that everything around you appears to be slowing down, which will, in turn, make it easier for you to relax. This does not mean the effect will kick in right away, however, as it may take several repetitions of the exercise before you start seeing any results. If you find yourself having trouble making it through the exercise for the allotted time, worry not, it will get easier with practice.

Breathing exercises such as this one help to minimize the manifestation of physical symptoms, and are extremely useful as they can be used at any time, regardless of your current mental state. There is little that is required of you, or by you, to do this anywhere, which means there is little to forget in times of crisis. If you have trouble focusing enough on your breathing that you can count the seconds successfully, counting them out on your fingers can give you the focus you need to tune out the anxiety for a long enough time for the exercise to take effect.

DAY 6
PROGRESSIVE MUSCLE RELAXATION

Progressive muscle relaxation is a technique, like measured breathing, that can be used in the moment to deal with particularly bad anxiety flair ups. It involves tensing and then relaxing specific groups of muscles in turn, as a means of distracting your anxiety and short circuiting the loop that causes it to manifest in the first place. This is due to the fact that it is difficult for your body to maintain a tensed, anxious state, and a relaxed calm state at the same time. As such, if you feel an anxiety attack coming your way, a period of focused relaxation may be just what you need to cut it off at the pass. You may also find this type of exercise useful if you are having difficulty falling to sleep or sleeping through for long.

While you will eventually be able to use this exercise in the moment, until you get the hang of it you are going to want to find some place quiet where you can focus on the task at hand. Give yourself 15 to 20 minutes of practice time to start out, though once you into the routine of it you will likely be able to experience the same results in far less time. To start, you simply need to pick a specific part of your body and shift the entirety of your focus to it. This step will be the same regardless of which muscle group you are focusing on.

For example, if you wanted to start with your left hand, you would hold it out in front of you, so you can focus on it fully. Then, while breathing slowly, in and out, you are going to want to tense all the muscles in your hand as hard as possible, for between five and ten seconds. You should tense hard enough that the tension starts to feel uncomfortable by the point that the time is up, though you should obviously refrain from tensing so hard that you hurt yourself. The goal here is to fully focus all of the tension you are feeling in general into the tension you feel in your hand.

After you have finished tensing, you will then want to abruptly change course and relax the muscles you were focusing on (in this case your hand). You will now want to relax those muscles completely, feeling all of the tightness float out of your muscles, and from your mental state as well. You will want to go completely limp for this exercise to be effective, before then focusing on the difference between the two states.

This comparison is where the real results come into play as it will force your body to realize that it is now in a relaxed state, which means that the anxiety you are feeling can't exist, so it has to abate. You will want to remain in your relaxed state for between 15 and 20 seconds, before moving on to the next muscle group, if your anxiety has not yet abated.

DAY 7

TEACH YOUR ANXIETY TO RESPOND PROPERLY

Training your anxiety to respond to the right cues is the last of the exercises that should be practiced every day, or at least whenever the need arises. In order to get in a mindset where it feels as though your anxiety is yours to control, the first thing you need to understand is that it is the amount of anxiety that you feel at a given point and time that is the problem, not the fact that you feel anxiety in the first place. Your anxiety is supposed to be triggered whenever you need to be a little more alert, as your survival may be on the line in some scenarios. However, when it gets out of hand, it can quickly go from helping to harming, which is why you need to teach it when to manifest itself and when it is not required.

The secret here is that your anxiety only manifests itself when your body triggers the type of responses that indicate a threat, either real or imagined, is fast approaching. This means, that if you hope to train your anxiety to be effectively selective, you are going to need to be mindful to provide it with the sort of feedback it needs in order to understand that everything is currently fine. To do this effectively, the first thing you want to do is to assess the types of responses, mental and physical, you are experiencing the next time you feel an onslaught of anxiety approaching.

Once you can determine what types of physical triggers are likely setting off your anxiety, you will be able to more easily determine how not to act in the future, if you hope to keep your anxiety in check. If you can manage to do this successfully, then you will be able to convince your anxiety that everything is fine and that it should calm down. This means you are going to want to prioritize open body language, a calm, measured speaking voice, keeping a smile on your face, regular breathing and making yourself salivate.

While it might seem silly, the truth of the matter is that if you can manage to adopt just one of these behaviors when you are feeling anxious you can likely alter your fear response enough to tell your body that everything is perfectly fine. One of the easiest ways to do so is simply by chewing gum, or even simply pretending that you are doing so, whether or not you have anything in your mouth at the moment.

What makes this trick so effective is that doing so causes your body to stop and take a moment to consider what is actually going on. After all, if you are salivating then you must be eating and if you are calmly eating then there must be nothing to worry about. This dramatic change to the feedback loop when compared to what your body was expecting should shut down your anxiety in short order; and, even better, you will find that knowing that you have this trick in your pocket can make you less anxious over all as well.

DAY 8

LOOK AT UNDERLYING ASSUMPTIONS

Generally speaking, when you feel anxious going into a given situation it is because you are afraid of the potential consequences, either real or imagined, that would naturally go along with the situation in question turning out badly. As such, if you hope to get to a point where you can face similar situations without feeling anxious, you will need to trace those fears back to their roots. Once there, you will often find that they don't have nearly the power that you previously expected them to, because the limits of what can happen have been defined.

As an example, assume that you are nervous about an important client meeting that is coming up, looking closer at this fear might, in turn, might reveal a fear of failure. Tracing this fear back you may then discover that it is based around an association that a failure leads to other, more serious consequences due to something that you experienced in the past. However, if you then really think about failure, you can realize that it is something that happens to everyone and that while there may be consequences to failure, it is hardly the end of the world.

Once you get to the true heart of the matter you will have a better idea of what is causing your anxiety, which means you can then more easily consider the true problem with a critical eye and determine if there is more to do when it comes to solving the issue you have been avoiding. In this instance, you may want to remind yourself of times where you have failed previously, and in many cases the results were relatively benign.

Once you understand that the root of the anxiety you are feeling isn't based in reality, you will then be free to discount all of the more fantastical reasons your mind has to be anxious. While it would be nice for the meeting to go well, for example, if it goes poorly it is unlikely that you will lose your job, your home or the respect of your family, so you can cross the more severe things off of your list of possible consequences right away. Finally, with that done, you will then be free to consider what may actually happen if things don't go according to plan and by this point the alternatives that you come up with will likely be far more benign than what you previously conjured in your mind, which will make it far more difficult to feel anxious about them.

This exercise has also proven especially effective for those who are having a hard time dealing with anxiety related to their relationship issues, as they can take the opportunity to describe all of the anxieties they have associated with fears that the relationship is going to fall apart. Often, while expressing these fears, those who are dealing with them will come to understand that their lives will ultimately continue as normal if the relationship falls apart. What's more, they will realize that the relationship in no way defines them as a person.

DAY 9

NIGHTMARE EXPOSURE AND RESCRIPTING

The next few days are going to focus on various types of exposure therapy that have been known to help anxiety that is brought on by various types of traumatic experiences in the past. Nightmare exposure and rescripting is a technique that has proven especially effective for those who are dealing with anxiety as a result of some type of post-traumatic stress disorder (PTSD).

Habitual nightmares can trigger anxiety related to sleep, and this can lead to additional disorders, in addition to making general anxiety of all types more severe, as the body is already running in a compromised state. This prolonged sleep debt can lead to a reduction in cognitive function levels, memory lapses and emotional instability, which will, in turn, lead to an increase in the presentation of anxiety symptoms.

When done correctly, nightmare exposure and rescripting combine the traditional ideas behind exposure therapy with additional emotional processing of the core event, to reduce the overall anxiety that is felt about the situation in question, and thus the ancillary incidents as well. The first step is going to be the most difficult, as it is going to involve looking back at the inciting incident and deciding what about it is the cause of the issues that have developed as a consequence of it.

The specific issues that you uncover are going to be different for everyone, and you may need professional help to deal with them properly. When you are ready to successfully unpack the issue, however, you are going to have to confront the dream repeatedly. You will want to start by writing down an account of the dream, not as it typically occurs, but as you would like it to occur instead. Rather than taking a turn for the worse, write out a narrative that sees the dream play out in a positive, if uneventful way. You are going to want to write this narrative right before you fall asleep, and be sure to physically write it out, to give the idea some extra substance.

Finally, all that is left to do is go to sleep. While it is unlikely that the first time that you write down your dream it is going to do you any good, you will find that with practice you will, slowly but surely, start to see more of your dream play out the way it does in your narrative. You are going to want to continue to write down the script for the dream every night, and make sure not to get discouraged if you have success at one point and then backslide. You have been having the dream for a prolonged period of time, it isn't going to change without a dedicated commitment to the idea.

DAY 10
IMAGERY BASED EXPOSURE

The goal of imagery based exposure is for you to react to the scenes that are presented as if they are actually occurring. While you might not think an image or memory can produce anxious results, with practice you will be surprised at how much of an effect they can have on your behavior. This type of exposure therapy is known to be particularly effective for those who are dealing with generalized anxiety disorder.

Imagery based exposure is particularly effective for those who find themselves ruminating on events in the past and building up their overall level of anxiety as a result. As such, it is typically effective when it comes to reducing the need to avoid high anxiety situations thanks to a lack of other, successful, coping mechanisms.

One version of this type of therapy is completed by bringing to mind a recent experience that caused strong feelings of anxiety as a result. For example, imagine you had recently given a presentation during a meeting for work. Using imagery exposure, you would then call up that situation in your mind and do your best to remember it as clearly as possible. Usually, it happens that our least favorite memories become burned in our brains, so you should have no trouble planting yourself firmly in the shoes of the you from the past.

For example, you would want to remember how the room looked, what your peers and your supervisor were wearing, what it felt like in the room, the sound it made when that one guy farted and tried to pass it off as a sneeze, anything that you can remember to place yourself as fully in the moment as possible. Once you have worked your way through the entire memory at least once, you will then want to run through it one more time, but this time take extra time to consider the thoughts and level of anxiety you had throughout the event, as well as any behavioral urges you may have had as well.

Once you have established a baseline for the level of anxiety that you felt during the conversation in question, you will then want to run through the memory from start to finish once more until the intensity of your anxiety drops by half or until you are no longer able to focus on the memory as clearly as you were at the start. You will then want to repeat the process at least once a day until you are able to get through the entire memory without even a twinge of anxiety.

Once you reach this point with the memory you started with, it is important to not rest on your laurels, as all the progress in the world on one high-anxiety incident is only going to do so much for any of the other times when you experience high levels of anxiety. Only by moving through all of your trigger experiences, one at a time, will you be able to move forward with a more anxiety free life.

DAY 11

EXPOSURE AND RESPONSE PREVENTION

Learning to gradually face the things that make you anxious is one of the most effective ways to put a negative thought cycle to rest for good. The exposure and response prevention exercise works by exposing you to an increasingly severe list of things that make you anxious, so that you are able to deal with your fears slowly but surely. Even better, it will also help you to stop needing any of unhealthy coping mechanisms you have likely developed over the years as well.

To get started in this process, the first thing you will need to do is to take a closer look at the things that make you anxious or anything that triggers the negative avoidance behaviors that you have created, in order to avoid facing the issue head on. This means you are going to want to refer back to your journal, or start keeping track of your triggers moving forward for a whole week. If you find that you are regularly dealing with more triggers than you can easily keep track of in a day, then starting with the big three each day is a perfectly valid option. You will then want to go ahead and give each trigger a severity rating on a scale from 1 to 10. Finally, you will want to take note of any coping strategies that you are currently using, regardless of whether these are negative or positive.

Once you have labeled all of your triggers, you are going to want to put them in order, starting with the mildest and increasing all the way up to the triggers that you can't get within a mile of without experiencing a serious anxiety attack. Once your list is created, if you weren't able to come up with a list that naturally starts at one and goes all the way to 10, then you are going to want to think hard and try and come up with triggers to fill the scale completely. This way you will be able to increase the level of anxiety that you feel with each event slowly but surely, to ensure that you don't end up accidentally biting off more than you can chew all at once.

When moving through this exercise, it is extremely important that you take things slowly, and only move onto the next trigger once you can experience the previous trigger without worrying about it in the slightest. Make sure that you hit every item on your list in order, as skipping ahead won't help you face your issues faster, and could even actually set you back, as you will have to deal with the failure along with everything else. When you are making your way through your list, you are going to want to be sure to keep track of each of your improvements in your journal so that you can look back on all that you have done at any point in the future when new triggers have emerged, and you aren't sure if you can best them.

DAY 12
INTEROCEPTIVE EXPOSURE

If you experience anxiety related to specific bodily sensations, then interoceptive exposure might be an effective exercise to desensitize the anxiety in question. The typical means of dealing with these types of anxiety promoting events is usually avoidance, which obviously doesn't really solve the problem, and can actually make things far worse over time. Avoidance of this type typically leads to biased beliefs which can then go so far as to influence virtually every aspect of your life. As with the other types of exposure therapy, the goal here is to slowly force yourself to come face to face with the sensations in question, so that you can ultimately learn to manage them on a daily basis.

Breathing

- Rapidly breathe in and out, taking full breathes each time (1 minute)

- Hold your nose and breathe through a straw (2 minutes)

- Hold your breath (30 seconds)

Physical exercise

- Run in place (2 minutes)

- Walk up and down the stairs (2 minutes)

- Tense all the muscles in your body (1 minute)

Spinning or shaking

- Spin as fast as you can while sitting in an office chair (1 minute)

- Spin while standing as fast as you can (1 minute)

- Shake your head back and forth before looking straight ahead (30 seconds)

- Put your head between your legs and then stand up quickly (1 minute)

- Lie down for a minute and then stand up quickly (1 minute)

- Stare at yourself in a mirror (2 minutes)

- Stare at a blank wall (2 minutes)

- Stare at a florescent light and then read something (1 minute)

If you find yourself having difficultly dealing with all of the exercises in question, all at once, it is perfectly fine to start with a small portion of them and work your way up to the full amount. Likewise, if you reach the end of the suggested exercises but still find that you are having issues with the sensation out in the real world, then you may want to include exercises based around those experiences or simply up the time limits on the above listed exercises, the most important thing is that the exercises work for you and your personalized needs.

When you first start the exercises, it is important to do so at a point where you will be able to complete them regularly, if not every day then at least several days per week. Repetition is key here, as only practicing once in a while will stress you out and not do you any good as a result. Depending on the severity of your anxiety, the early days of this exercise could be extremely slow going. This is perfectly alright, there is no timetable for how long this exercise should take, the right speed is the speed at which you improve your tolerance to the sensations that cause you the most anxiety.

DAY 13
SEEK OUT NEGATIVE THINKING TRAPS

By now it should be clear to you that your thoughts affect not only the way in which you see yourself but the world around you as well. While this normally isn't much of an issue or concern, if your anxiety has progressed to the point where you have developed the types of thinking traps, or cognitive distortions, discussed in Chapter 1, then this exercise will help you to excise them from your mind once and for all.

This exercise is going to use coping statements to help you to convince your mind that you are able to deal with the situations that your cognitive distortions see as untenable, to the point where the distortions fade into the background. When it comes to ensuring that they help to lower your anxiety, it is important that your coping statement be as personalized to your situation as possible. What follows are a number of example coping statements to help point you in the right direction.

If your anxious thought is that you are never going to improve at a skill or activity that you want to improve at, then you could replace this thought with a more productive thought such as:

- I have made changes before and can do so again.

- I have a support system in place that will help me through this difficult time.

- I have to simply take things one day at a time.

- Don't beat yourself up, at least you are trying.

If your anxious thought has to do with the assumption that anything that you eat is going to immediately cause you to gain weight, then you could replace this thought with a more productive thought such as:

- No one food has that amount of power over me.

- There are plenty of healthy reasons to eat this particular item of food.

- A vast majority of foods are fine in moderation.

- One of these is not going to make me gain weight.

Other useful coping statements include:

- Just go for it.

- Taking time for myself is perfectly acceptable.

- My anxiety does not define me.

- Food is fuel.

- I am smart, health and strong.

- I am capable of making good choices.

- My life is mine to do with as I will.

- Practice makes perfect.

- In 10 years' time this will not matter.

- I deserve respect.

- My thoughts do not define my reality.

- The worst-case scenario practically never occurs.

- My best will be good enough for the vast majority of situations.

- Being anxious will not prevent me from tackling this situation head on.

- I have time for me.

- I deserve a break.

- Practice, practice, practice.

- I can face the fear.

- I can choose to think different thoughts.

- I am in control of my mind.

- I deserve to feel happy.

- This is not that big of a deal, I will not let it get to me.

- Breathe deeply.

- I am in the right place, at the right time, exactly where I need to be.

- The future is not set in stone.

DAY 14

CONSIDER YOUR CORE BELIEFS

If you have been dealing with anxiety for your entire life, then it is entirely possible that some facet of your core belief system may be fundamentally incongruous with the way the world works. The first step in ensuring that this is no longer the case, while also decreasing your overall level anxiety in the process, is to determine what mental agreements are coming into play. These mental agreements typically come in bundles which means that if you take the time to identify the package of beliefs that you are interacting with, you will be well on your way to changing them, which will be covered in tomorrow's exercise.

As with many of the exercises discussed in these pages, it may be difficult to pull off correctly at first but will get easier with practice. In order to get started effectively you may find it useful to think of uncovering a core belief as akin to solving a mystery, which means you need to get to look at the clues that are left in place by your subconscious.

For example, if the thought of speaking in public is enough to make you extremely anxious, then your fear of public speaking is not really the issue. Likewise, if the reason that this makes you anxious is that you are afraid that people are going to assume you are not intelligent if you do speak in public then this is an emotional reaction to a belief, not a belief itself. Fears associated with the opinions that other people may have about you, are one of the most common triggers for anxiety that there is, this same essential dynamic also occurs when asking for anything that you want, from a date to a raise.

It is important to learn to distinguish these types of thoughts from core beliefs as your thoughts are not to be trusted if you are dealing with an extreme level of anxiety disorder. When it comes to tracking down the core belief that is causing you anxiety in the moment, the best way to continue digging deeper is to follow the emotions that you are having in response. You will want to continue to question how your emotions are being influenced by external events to get to the core belief that is truly pulling the strings.

Regardless of what core belief is at play in your situation, it is important to keep in mind that external factors such as the things other people think about you won't affect your anxiety if you don't share the same deep-rooted assumption about yourself that is manifesting through your anxiety. As such, if you look back to the previous example, then if you find that you are made anxious at the thought of public speaking because you were afraid that other people might think you are not intelligent, then you may need to consider this fear more deeply, as it is possible that your core belief is tied to it in one way or another.

DAY 15
CHANGE YOUR CORE BELIEFS

Once you have determined the core beliefs that are causing you undue anxiety, the next step is going to be banishing them from your thought processes once and for all. While the deeply internalized nature of the belief, in the example from the previous chapter this was a core belief that you were not intelligent, can be a difficult nut to crack, you can begin softening it up by first considering the way you deal with the assumptions of others.

Most importantly, this means coming to the understanding that you cannot ever be exactly how people see you in their heads. While somewhat of a letdown, this idea should be largely mitigated by the fact that you can't ever truly know what another person is thinking, so you will never know what you are actually up against. This is an easy truth to come to, after all, you are not a mind reader; nevertheless, it is powerful in that it puts some space to work in the set of beliefs that are tied directly to the core belief you are going to change. Becoming aware of the limits of your beliefs can make them much easier to change.

It is also important to keep in mind that you don't need to change the entire bundle of agreements that make up the core belief all at once. Each agreement can be thought of as a link in a chain, which means you only need to weaken a handful of the links before the chain can no longer remain intact. One of the weakest links in many of these types of chains is the belief that because someone else thinks something about you, this obviously makes it true, which is something that many people believe, often without thinking twice about it.

This clearly starts to fall apart under any amount of scrutiny, however, as different people are always going to have opinions about us, but there is never a guarantee that these opinions or people are well-informed ones. This process then becomes even more nebulous when you consider the fact that they may have their own cognitive distortions in play, that may render their opinion of you completely invalid.

Once you make the leap and begin understanding that you are more than a mental concept in someone else's mind, you will find that many other beliefs that are based on other people's views begin to lose their power as well. If you are more than just a mental concept (you are) then what other people think about you becomes significantly less important, and it certainly means that they can't do anything to hurt you emotionally as well.

Once you reach this point, you will realize that changing a core belief is actually extremely easy, all you need to do is to stop believing the old version and start believing the new version instead. The only thing you really need to learn is how to identify them, which should get easier every time you do it successfully. All that is left in order to improve your core beliefs for the better is to shift your point of view.

DAY 16
SHIFT YOUR POINT OF VIEW

Once you have come face to face with your core beliefs, the only thing left to do in order to change them for good is going to be shifting your point of view to ensure that all the work you have done over the past few days locks into place. A new perspective will make it easier for you to have an epiphany when it comes to the way you see the world in general, and shake your core beliefs to their foundations in the process.

If you don't take this final step and ensure you have properly shifted your perspective, it is very difficult to change a belief in the long-term. This is because when you remain in the paradigm that the false belief created, the belief naturally seems true, which makes it easy to continue to believe it. Like someone who believes the earth is flat, this paradigm makes it easy to ignore evidence to the contrary, regardless of how compelling that evidence might be.

In order to change your perspective successfully, you are going to want to start by considering the situation that you feel most embodies the aspects of the belief that causes you anxiety in the first place. Once you have selected this activity or situation, this next part is going to be rather painful, even if you are well on your way to purging the core belief from your life. You are going to want to experience the event that causes you anxiety, and enlist the aid of someone else to film you while you complete whatever it is that was causing your anxiety. If you are lucky enough to have an existing recording of yourself doing that thing, then you can skip the repeat performance.

Once you have the recording in hand, the next step is going to be to watch it, not as if you were watching a recording of yourself, but as if you are watching a recording of a stranger that you stumbled across on YouTube. This will give you a different perspective on the entire proceedings and show you that you have nothing to be anxious over in regard to this particular scenario. Even if you make a mistake, or otherwise confirm your anxiety in your own eyes, if you watch carefully you will notice that those around you likely don't react at all, and almost certainly, at least without any open hostility.

While on the surface, this is nothing that you did not experience firsthand, in the moment, you will be surprised what watching it unfold before you, instead of experiencing it happening to you, can do for your perception. Likewise, once you have experienced an unfiltered perspective on the action, you will find that it is nearly impossible to believe something that you have physically seen disproven with your own eyes. If your core belief doesn't change right away, a few repeat viewings should put it to rest for good.

DAY 17

RECONSIDER COMMON PATTERNS

Once you have started to question the cognitive distortions that have built up in your mind as a result of your prolonged anxiety, you will likely notice that some of the common patterns that you move through during your day, as well as some of the common mental patterns that your mind moves through without you even taking notice, start seeming a little out of date. In order to break free from them once and for all, you are going to need to focus on the negative habits that they are associated with.

While it can be difficult to break habits that have been formed over years, if not decades, as a way to deal with an anxiety, a good place to start is by questioning the validity of habits that you naturally assume are beneficial to you in some way, shape or form. The easiest way to go about doing so, is to simply call them out on their bluff.

For example, if your anxiety makes it difficult for you to take breaks while you are working, under the assumption that not taking breaks makes a person more efficient overall, then the easiest way to put this habit to the test is by simply measuring how long it takes for you to complete common tasks, both based on the way you work currently and an alternate schedule where you take regular breaks. Then, you would have all of the data you need to properly assess the situation, without any guess work coming into play at all.

Even after you have gone ahead and disproven the efficacy of a particular habit, that doesn't mean that it is immediately going to disappear, far from it. This is due to the way the brain works, which is by sending the neurons that cause thoughts to become actions along the pathways in your mind that have the least resistance. The more common a pattern is, the less resistance its pathway is going to have. As such, in order to change a habit successfully, you are going to want to start by making small changes that won't represent a dramatic shift to the pathway all at once.

For example, if you want to eat healthier, going from eating junk food to eating salads for every meal isn't going to stick no matter how good your intentions. Instead, you are going to want to switch to healthier products that mimic unhealthy foods first, so that the neural pathway can accept the basics of the change before leaning on it too heavily. While this is a good start towards changing your patterns for good, it is important to keep it up once the change starts, and not partially alter the habit and call it good. Any trace of the existing neural pathway is going to be enough for your anxiety to creep back in and continue to interfere with your life, a total shift is the only way to see the success you are looking for.

DAY 18

PUT YOUR THOUGHTS ON TRIAL

Depending on the type of cognitive distortion that you are dealing with, you may find a more direct, confrontational approach to be an effective way of forcing your anxiety into submission. For this exercise, you are essentially going to hold the thoughts that are causing your anxiety on trial. To ensure things are fair, you are going to be acting as both the prosecution, the defense, the jury and the executioner.

When getting started with this exercise, the best way to go about doing so is going to be as the defense, so you can determine how best to attack the distortion as the prosecution. As the defense, you job is going to be coming up with legitimate, non-emotional arguments as to why the thought based on the cognitive distortion in question may actually be valid. Only cold hard facts should be allowed into your mental courtroom, if you can't back up an argument with something that you don't just think to be true, but that you positively know to be true, then you are not allowed to enter it into evidence.

Make sure you act as the judge during this period as well, to ensure that this rule is strictly adhered too, and that you, as the defense, do a reasonable job of defending your client (your thought patterns). While your overall goal should be to disprove the distortion, it is important that you don't skip this step and move straight to the prosecution arguments. The goal here is not to bully your mind into accepting the truth, it is to show your thoughts the error of their ways through cold, hard, facts. If you railroad the defense then this will ultimately make it easier for the anxiety to return, not more difficult.

Once the defense has had their turn, it will then be time to attack the distortion that you are dealing with using all of the facts and logic at your disposal. As the distortion is likely grasping at straws when it comes to remaining an accurate reflection of reality, this should be a relatively easy task. That doesn't mean that you can shirk your role as the prosecution, however, again, the point is to get your mind to confront the disparities directly, just assuming that the prosecution is going to win out misses the point of the exercise as a whole.

As the jury, it is your job to weigh the arguments on both sides and come to a conclusion, based on the strength of each argument. This is your chance to look at the arguments both for and against the cognitive distortion, laid bare. If there was ever a question in your mind, even a slight one, that things might not be as they seem then this should set you straight. Who knows, the distortion might have a grain of truth to it after all. Finally, all that is left is for you to act as the executioner for the cognitive distortion in question and banish it from your mind for good.

DAY 19

WRITING AND DESTROYING

One thing that has been lost in the transition to a largely digital world is the ability of a handwritten letter or note to change our perspective on something, and thus help with a variety of mental issues, including anxiety. There is significant benefit to laying your thoughts out in a physical space, so that you can reflect on them externally, without the internal filters that may cause them to become twisted or negative.

For the purpose of this exercise, you are going to be participating in what is known as transactional writing, which is writing with the purpose of exchanging feelings, beliefs and thoughts with another person, though you will be the target audience for this particular letter. You may write a letter to your former self, your future self, or an aspirational version of yourself that can be viewed more as an ambitious goal.

When writing, it is important to observe the common conventions that go along with a traditional letter such as a common greeting and a closing. When writing a letter to another person, it is natural to become more conscious of the other person, and it is this consciousness that you are striving to get in touch with along the way. Getting a feel for the version of yourself that you are writing a letter to will allow you to express all the hopes and fear you have for yourself, along with all of the anxiety you have over the past, future or aspirational version of yourself that you are striving for.

While you are writing to yourself, try and consider what this other version of you would have to say about the letter you are writing. Coming at the experiences you are expressing from another direction may make it easier to understand where the issues lie, and possibly what can be done to make them more manageable. This type of writing is particularly effective when it comes to dealing with the ancillary emotions that come along with your anxiety, in addition to the anxiety itself. While writing, you are going to want to go on for as long as you feel the need, cutting yourself off before you are finished will only leave unresolved issues floating around, making it more likely your anxiety will return.

Once you have gotten everything out of your system as thoroughly as possible, you are then going to want to destroy the paper in the way that seems most appropriate to you. It is important that you do more than simply discard the letter. The process should be somewhat more elaborate than that, as a way of giving the anxiety that is contained within it the send off it deserves. The goal is to have a destruction ceremony that you will be able to easily recall in the future, if your issues return. If the anxiety does try to creep back, simply picture the destruction ceremony in your mind and remind yourself that these issues have been dealt with.

DAY 20

TRACK THE FLUID NATURE
OF YOUR FEELINGS

While working through the exercises in this book, there is naturally a significant discussion of feelings, and their interplay with both actions and thoughts. While changing your feelings of anxiety can be difficult, when you come at them directly, it is important to keep in mind that they are naturally going to change on their own over time as well. As such, no matter how much a given situation makes you anxious at the moment, it is important to always remember that nothing is set in stone and that change is always possible.

While this is easy to say, and even to believe on a general level, focusing that belief on the things that make you anxious is much easier said than done. As such, the exercise for today is going to consist of looking back through the journal entries you have created since day one and considering how you feel now about the things that have been making you anxious for at least the past few weeks.

While some of these things are likely still going to be causing you a fair amount of anxiety, odds are you will be surprised by how many of the things that recently made you anxious, now don't even warrant a second thought.

On the other side of the coin, it is important to keep in mind that it has only been a few weeks, which means it is important to not expect too much too soon. Just because you have put in serious work for a few weeks, doesn't mean that your anxiety is going to disappear completely and never return. In fact, this is likely never going to be the case entirely, as new anxiety triggers are bound to manifest themselves from time to time.

Instead, when you do come across new instances of anxiety, it is important to react to it in a reasonable fashion and not blow its presence out of proportion. Overreacting to the fact that you have once again become anxious about a specific type of situational anxiety that you have previously largely conquered is only going to make the entire experience more difficult to deal with, than if you had just properly taken things in your stride in the first place. You may find it helpful to verbally acknowledge what you are going through, and frame the sentence in a positive way, so that the additional anxiety seems like little more than a bump in the road. For example, you might say, "Currently I'm feeling a little anxious, which is natural given the situation. When the feeling passes I anticipate feeling clear headed and calm once more."

Additionally, you are going to need to simply accept the fact that you are likely always going to be somewhat more anxious than other people, and instead of fighting that fact, focus on keeping it contained as much as possible. Otherwise constantly fighting this truth is akin to simply letting the anxiety win, and by this part you have come much to far for that to be a realistic option.

DAY 21
KEEP IT UP

When it comes to improving your response to anxiety in the long-term, it is important to find those exercises that work best for you and to stick with them regularly for a long enough period of time that your mind and body begins to get used to the new habits. While you will likely find yourself feeling somewhat out of sorts, at first, once your mind and body learn what to expect going forward, you will discover that the process is actually much easier than you originally anticipated it would be. Additionally, sticking to a routine of exercises will help you to begin to see the results of your hard work appearing sooner, which will do wonders for your motivation as well.

On the other hand, if you dither about when it comes to improving your response to anxiety and try various different exercises, but only practice them on odd occasions rather than routinely, then instead of enhancing your body's natural ability to limit anxiety, you will find that things are more chaotic than ever. If you hope to see any results in the long term, the only way to ensure this happens is to find a handful of CBT methods that work for you and stick with them until you find the results you seek.

With that being said, just because you miss a few days of exercises, now and then, it is no reason to throw in the towel and give up on any hard work you have put in up until that point. While constant repetition is going to generate better results, that doesn't mean there still isn't plenty that you can benefit from by using a more relaxed schedule. The only time you should feel guilty about missing a scheduled exercise time is if you purposely scheduled something during the time to get out of what you need to do in order to beat your anxiety, deliberate avoidance, or if you use the fact that you missed a day or two of exercises as an excuse to miss even more. As long as you spend more days making forward progress than you do falling behind, then you are sure to meet your goals eventually.

There is enough working against you when it comes to actively fighting off your anxiety. Don't add more to your plate by sabotaging your success as well. If you are actively working towards your overall goal you are sill doing far more than otherwise might be the case, which means there is nothing to beat yourself up over.

The same goes for the length of time that may pass by before you start seeing any real success. Just remember, it took you quite a long time to get to the mental state that you are currently in. There is no reason to expect the changes develop and succeed overnight. Always remember, that when it comes to improving your anxiety, the process is a marathon, not a sprint, which means that slow and steady is going to win the race.

CONCLUSION

Thank you for making it through to the end of *Cognitive Behavioral Therapy: A 21 Day Step by Step Guide to Overcoming Anxiety, Depression & Negative Thought Patterns - Simple Methods to Retrain Your Brain.* Let's hope it was informative and able to provide you with all of the tools you need to achieve your goals. Just because you've finished this book doesn't mean there is nothing left to learn on the topic; expanding your horizons is the only way to find the mastery you seek.

Likewise, while the exercises in this book will offer you a great leg up when it comes to shaping your anxiety into a more manageable form, they are by no means everything that can be done when it comes to using CBT to combat your anxiety. If you feel as though you have reached the end of what you can do for yourself, then rest assured that there is still more that can be gained by seeking out a therapist who specializes in CBT to take you through a guided CBT session. While you will likely go over many of the exercises discussed here, having a guiding hand to move you through the process is sure to provide you with additional insight that you may not be able to discover on your own.

Above all else, it is important to remember that you are ultimately in control of your anxiety, not the other way around. Believing that there is a solution out there for you is the first step towards actually doing something about it. Keep a positive attitude and you are sure to find a solution that works for you as long as you believe that success is possible.

Finally, if you found this book useful in any way, a review is always appreciated!

Made in the USA
Coppell, TX
20 November 2019

11656801R00049